SAINT. What is the [...] you hear this word? [...] name such as St. Aug[...] ine of Siena? We are [...] grateful to have such models of holiness to draw inspiration from. But can you think of anyone a bit closer in your life, in your circle of friends or acquaintances, or within your family even, that may reflect the life or virtues of a saint?

Mother Teresa once said "holiness is not the luxury of a few people, but a simple duty for you and me. We have been created for that." If this shocks you, it shouldn't. If perfection is the premise upon which we decide if someone is holy, I'm afraid not too many people – none, really – will make the cut. Even the prominent saints that we have admired for so long had real human struggles. When we lose focus of their *whole* humanity, the good and the bad, we make it impossible for us to think of sainthood as something achievable in our own lives.

What makes the saints extraordinary people is that they made their lives bigger than themselves by uniting themselves

to the will of God in their lives. As you read through this book, may these brothers and sisters of ours in Christ help us to transform our own lives into something extraordinary as well.

Natalia Kononenko
Editor, *Living with Christ*

Prayer:
Conversing with God

*Acquire the habit of speaking to God
as if you were alone with him,
familiarly and with confidence and love,
as to the dearest and most loving of friends.*
—St. Alphonsus Liguori

Saint Alphonsus Liguori

THE LIFE OF ALPHONSUS LIGUORI (1696-1787) spanned the 18th century. Born in Naples, he was ordained in 1726. He soon won a reputation in Naples as a preacher and became widely sought as a confessor. He was committed to preaching sermons that were simple to understand and structured to hold the listener's attention. In 1732 he went to Scala and founded an order of mission priests that became the Redemptorists. His *Moral Theology* was published in 1748.

Alphonsus was known for his great kindness and concern for others. Made a bishop in 1762, he retired in 1775. He was canonized in 1839 and in 1871 was named a Doctor of the Church. St. Alphonsus Liguori is a patron of moral theologians and confessors.

When we stand praying...
we ought to be watchful and earnest
with our whole heart,
intent on our prayers.
Let all carnal and worldly thoughts pass away,
nor let the soul at that time think of anything
except the object of its prayer.
—ST. ALOYSIUS GONZAGA

Saint Aloysius Gonzaga

ALOYSIUS GONZAGA (1568-91) is a patron saint of young men. Born a prince in Lombardy, Aloysius began to practise prayer and penance at a young age, rejecting the values of his position and family. Against great resistance, in 1585 he gave up his rights as eldest son and joined the Jesuits, hoping to go to the missions. Instead, in 1591 the plague broke out in Rome, and Aloysius offered himself to serve the sick and dying in the hospital. He caught the plague and died three months later, at just 23 years old. He was canonized in 1726.

A soul arms itself by prayer for all kinds of combat.
In whatever state the soul may be, it ought to pray. [...]
There is no soul that is not bound to pray, for every
single grace comes to the soul through prayer.
—St. Faustina Kowalska

Saint Faustina Kowalska

BORN IN THE VILLAGE OF GŁOGOWIEC, near Lodz, in Poland in 1905, and dying in Kraków in 1938, Saint Faustina spent her short life amongst the Sisters of Our Lady of Mercy, generously conforming herself to the vocation she received from God and developing an intense spiritual life, rich in spiritual gifts and in faithful harmony with them.

In the *Diary* of her soul, Faustina herself recounts what the Lord worked in her for the benefit of all: listening to him who is love and mercy, she understood that no human wretchedness could measure itself against the mercy which ceaselessly pours from the heart of Christ. Thus she became the inspiration for a movement dedicated to proclaiming and imploring Divine Mercy throughout the whole world.

Canonized in the year 2000 by Saint John Paul II, the name of Faustina quickly became known around the world, thereby promoting the invocation of Divine Mercy and its credible witness in the conduct of the lives of believers. St. Faustina Kowalska is a patron saint of mercy. *(source: vatican.va)*

Prayer is the best weapon we have;
it is the key to God's heart.
You must speak to Jesus not only with your lips,
but with your heart. In fact on certain occasions you
should only speak to him with your heart.
—ST. PIUS OF PIETRELCINA

Saint Pius of Pietrelcina

FRANCESCO FORGIONE (1887-1968) was born in the Italian village of Pietrelcina. He entered the novitiate of the Capuchin Friars at the age of 16, taking the name Pio ('pious'), and was ordained in 1910. A stigmatic, he lived more than 50 years at the friary of San Giovanni Rotondo, devoted to a life of ministry through sacramental reconciliation and celebration of the Eucharist, and helping countless people who sought his counsel.

Pope Paul VI said of him: "Look what fame he had, what a worldwide following gathered around him! But why? Perhaps because he was a philosopher? Because he was wise? Because he had resources at his disposal? Because he said Mass humbly, heard confessions from dawn to dusk and was – it is not easy to say it – one who bore the wounds of our Lord. He was a man of prayer and suffering." Padre Pio was canonized by Pope John Paul II in 2002.

Do you wish to rise?
Begin by descending.
You plan a tower that will pierce the clouds?
Lay first the foundation of humility.
—St. Augustine

Saint Augustine

Born in North Africa, Saint Augustine lived from 354 to 430. He went to university at Carthage to study rhetoric but became interested in philosophy and literature instead. Augustine taught in North Africa for several years and then opened a school of rhetoric in Rome, moving to Milan in 384. There he heard the sermons of Bishop Ambrose and became convinced of the truth of Christianity. During Easter 387, Augustine was baptized by Ambrose and he and his entourage went to North Africa. In 391, the people of Hippo, near his hometown of Tagaste, insisted Augustine be ordained. Priest and ascetic, he established a religious community and began preaching. In 396, he became bishop of Hippo, where he spent the rest of his life.

These events and many more are recounted in Augustine's *Confessions,* a classic of spiritual autobiography. His other writings include *City of God, De trinitate (On the Trinity),* and *De doctrina christiana (On Christian Doctrine).* He is one of the greatest Fathers of the Church, known as the Doctor of Grace.

Build an oratory within yourself,
and here have Jesus
on the altar of your heart.

—ST. PAUL OF THE CROSS

Saint Paul of the Cross

PAUL OF THE CROSS was a "walking saint": when he walked in public, crowds pressed in on him, hoping to get a piece of his habit as a relic, or to ask for a cure or a favour.

Born in northern Italy in 1694, Paul experienced conversion at 15 and began a lifetime's devotion to prayer and austerity. After having had several visions, he determined that his vocation was to found an order dedicated to the Passion of our Lord. Officials declared the visions authentic and Paul withdrew to write a rule. He was joined by his brother, who remained with him for the rest of his life.

By 1747, the Passionists had three houses and were preaching missions throughout Italy. At his death in 1775, Paul was establishing a congregation for Passionist nuns. St. Paul of the Cross was canonized in 1867.

> *More tears are shed over answered prayers*
> *than unanswered ones.*
> **—St. Teresa of Avila**

Saint Teresa of Avila

TERESA WAS BORN IN AVILA, Spain, on March 28, 1515, and died in 1582. Of the many women who have exercised leadership roles in the Church, Teresa must surely be considered among the greatest.

When she entered the Carmelite convent, some thought Teresa was a spoiled young woman with an unremarkable prayer life but she soon advanced in prayer, experiencing visions and hearing voices. Dissatisfied with the laxity she perceived among religious, she determined to institute reforms and established St. Joseph's Convent where enclosure and a strict rule prevailed. With the assistance of Peter of Alcantara and John of the Cross, Teresa succeeded in founding the reformed (Discalced) Carmelite orders of nuns and friars.

Teresa wrote several works considered classics of spiritual literature, including *The Way of Perfection* and *The Interior Castle*. A great mystic and a strong, intelligent and active leader, Teresa was canonized in 1622 and in 1970 became the first woman to be declared a Doctor of the Church. She is a patron of Spain.

> *The limitless loving devotion to God, and the gift God makes of himself to you, are the highest elevation of which the heart is capable; it is the highest degree of prayer. The souls that have reached this point are truly the heart of the Church.*
>
> —St. Teresa Benedicta of the Cross

Saint Teresa Benedicta of the Cross

EDITH STEIN was born in Breslau, Germany (present-day Wrocław, Poland) on October 12, 1891, the youngest child in a large Jewish family. She studied philosophy with Edmund Husserl and received her doctorate at age 25. Drawn to Catholicism, Edith was baptized in 1922 and spent the next 12 years teaching at Catholic institutions. In 1934 she joined the Carmelites in Cologne, taking the name Teresa Benedicta of the Cross. By 1938 anti-Semitism was widespread, and her prioress helped Edith flee the Nazis, escaping to the Netherlands. She continued her writing and studies until August 2, 1942, when she and her sister were arrested by the Gestapo.

On August 7, 987 Jews were deported to Auschwitz, and on August 9, Edith Stein, her sister and others died in the gas chambers. Although a convert to Catholicism, Edith Stein always acknowledged her Jewish heritage. Canonized on October 11, 1998, she is co-patron of Europe with Saints Benedict, Cyril and Methodius, Bridget of Sweden and Catherine of Siena.

> *When you kneel before an altar,*
> *do it in such a way*
> *that others may be able to recognize*
> *that you know before whom you kneel.*
> **—St. Maximilian Kolbe**

Saint Maximilian Kolbe

Saint Maximilian was born in Poland in 1894. As a Franciscan, he worked to spread the Gospel in his native Poland as well as in Japan. He had a great devotion to Our Lady.

During the Nazi occupation of Poland, he helped thousands of refugees, including Polish Jews. He was arrested by the Gestapo in 1941 and imprisoned at Auschwitz. Three months after Maximilian's arrival, a prisoner escaped. In retaliation, 10 men were chosen at random to die. One was a young father; Maximilian offered to take his place. His offer accepted, Maximilian died on this day in 1941 and was canonized in October 1982. He is a patron saint of prisoners and the pro-life movement.

When my faith is weak

A marvellous and mighty paradox
has thus occurred, for the death
which they thought to inflict on him
as dishonour and disgrace
has become the glorious monument
to death's defeat.
−St. Athanasius

Saint Athanasius

BORN AT ALEXANDRIA in Egypt about 297, Athanasius is one of the Greek Fathers and a Doctor of the Church. He was present at the Council of Nicaea (325), convened to oppose the Arian heresy, which denied the divinity of Christ. Bishop of Alexandria and spiritual head of the desert hermits and of Ethiopia, Athanasius was a brilliant and formidable defender of orthodoxy, incurring the wrath of a succession of non-Christian emperors who repeatedly forced him into exile.

Athanasius wrote several outstanding treatises on Catholic doctrine, especially on the Incarnation, and introduced monasticism to the West. He died in 373. Through his example, his learning and his writings, he remains one of our greatest teachers. St. Athanasius is a patron saint of theologians.

> *God watched over me*
> *before I knew him*
> *and before I learned sense*
> *or even distinguished between good and evil.*
> **–St. Patrick**

Saint Patrick

ALTHOUGH LEGENDS ABOUND concerning the life and work of Patrick, Apostle of Ireland, he tells us about himself in his *Confession*. At 16, Patrick was carried off from Wales in a pirate raid and sold as a slave in Ireland. He was made a swineherd, living in solitude on a mountain, where a life of prayer and asceticism marked him forever. After serving his master for six years, Patrick heard an inner voice tell him that he would return to his homeland, and he escaped. Landing in Gaul (Western Europe), Patrick had many adventures before reaching his parents in Britain. Later, he returned to Gaul to study for the priesthood, eventually becoming a bishop. When the missionary to Ireland, Saint Palladius, died, Patrick took his place. By the time of his death in 492, he could see the fruits of his work: a native clergy was in place, Christianity had reached nearly all of Ireland, and churches and monasteries had been established.

St. Patrick is a patron of Ireland and Nigeria, of engineers, of several Canadian dioceses, and of those who fear snakes.

> *For I do not seek to understand in order that I may believe, but I believe in order to understand. For this also I believe – that unless I believe I shall not understand.*
> –ST. ANSELM

Saint Anselm

BORN IN 1033, Anselm was motivated to enter the monastery of Bec in Normandy due to the reputation of the great teacher, Lanfranc. Anselm became a monk at the age of 27, and a student and close friend of Lanfranc, eventually succeeding him as prior and abbot of Bec.

After the Norman Conquest of England in 1066, William I replaced the English hierarchy with Normans, and Lanfranc was sent as archbishop of Canterbury. Three years after Lanfranc's death, Anselm was in England (1093) and was forcibly made archbishop. Neither an administrator nor a politician by nature, he persevered nonetheless. Through his encouragement of English devotions, he helped heal the wounds of the Conquest on the English.

Anselm's fame lies in his role as theologian and philosopher. His argument for the existence of God still holds strong appeal. In his concern for the oppressed, he was one of the first opponents of the slave trade.

Anselm died in 1109. Never formally canonized, he was made a Doctor of the Church in 1720.

*Our wish, our object, our chief preoccupation must
be to form Jesus in ourselves, to make his spirit,
his devotion, his affections, his desires,
and his disposition live and reign there.*

– St. John Eudes

Saint John Eudes

BORN IN NORMANDY IN 1601, Saint John Eudes joined the Paris Oratory and was ordained in 1625. Twice during outbreaks of the plague John tended the sick and dying. In 1641, he helped found a refuge for women. The Visitandines working at the refuge became the core of a new religious order for women: the Sisters of Our Lady of Charity of the Refuge, which today has many branches, including the Sisters of Our Lady of Charity of the Good Shepherd in Canada.

Seeing the urgent need for clerical reform, John left the Oratorians in 1643 to found the Congregation of Jesus and Mary, dedicated to upgrading the religious and intellectual formation of the clergy.

John died in 1680. In the decree of his beatification in 1908, Pope Pius X declared John Eudes to be the father, doctor and apostle of the devotions to the Sacred Heart of Jesus and to the Immaculate Heart of Mary. He was canonized in 1925.

Cast yourself with confidence into the arms of God.
And be very sure of this, that if he wants anything
of you, he will fit you for your work
and give you strength to do it.
—St. Philip Neri

Saint Philip Neri

PHILIP NERI was born in Florence in 1515. He experienced conversion at the age of 18 and left for Rome, where he studied philosophy and theology for three years before choosing to re-evangelize Rome. He spent his days talking to people about God's love, and his nights in prayer. In 1548 he helped found a confraternity of laymen to minister to needy pilgrims, leading to the establishment of a now-famous Roman hospital, Santa Trinità dei Pellegrini. In 1551, his confessor insisted Philip be ordained. Disciples flocked to him, and he founded the congregation of the Oratorians, which was formally approved in 1575. Pope Gregory XIII gave them an ancient church in Rome, which they rebuilt and occupy to this day.

Philip's sermons were famous for their wisdom and good humour. He said, "I will have no sad spirits in my house. Cheerful people are more easily led to perfection." He died at the age of 80, much loved and respected, and is still known as the "Apostle of Rome." St. Philip Neri is the patron of home missions, supported in Canada through the Catholic Missions in Canada.

*The greater and more persistent
your confidence in God,
the more abundantly you will receive
what you ask.*

—St. Albert the Great

Saint Albert the Great

BORN IN SWABIA ABOUT 1206, Albert was the son of a German count who objected to his son's joining the newly founded Dominican Order. Albert earned a doctorate from the University of Paris and taught theology there and in Cologne. Thomas Aquinas (1225-74), one of his students, became a close friend and fellow scholar.

Albert received the title "Great" from his contemporaries in recognition of his intellectual gifts. He developed original ideas, was an accomplished philosopher, scientist, theologian, administrator, and teacher, and a keen student of Arabic learning and culture. Albert is best known for adapting for theologians Aristotle's works in philosophy and logic. He initiated the Scholastic method (application of Aristotelian methods to Christian doctrine), developed at length by Thomas Aquinas. Albert died in 1280 and was declared a Doctor of the Church in 1931. He is a patron saint of scientists.

Let us pray for each other
that Our Lord may give us
the grace that we need
to become saints.

—ST. BERNADETTE SOUBIROUS

Saint Bernadette Soubirous

BERNADETTE SOUBIROUS was born in 1844 in Lourdes, France, the eldest of nine children. In childhood she was stricken with cholera, was a severe asthmatic, and suffered ill health throughout her brief life. At the age of 14, over a five-month period, she had visions of the Blessed Virgin Mary at a grotto near her home in Lourdes.

Bernadette's parents and the local people were initially sceptical, but Bernadette remained faithful to the visions and messages she had received from Our Lady, and in 1862 they were confirmed by both Church and French authorities. In 1866 Bernadette joined the Sisters of Charity and lived the rest of her life in prayer and humble service. She died in 1879 and was canonized in 1933.

St. Bernadette is a patron of illness, and the shrine built to Our Lady of Lourdes is a major Catholic pilgrimage site.

The more I follow him without fear,
the more he will protect me.
The more I do his will,
the more he will prove his love for me.
–ST. MARGUERITE BOURGEOYS

Saint Marguerite Bourgeoys

MARGUERITE is often referred to as the "Mother of the Colony" for her contributions to the establishment of Ville-Marie, the place known today as Montreal.

Born in France in 1620, Marguerite crossed the Atlantic in 1653 to join in the colonizing efforts begun by Monsieur de Maisonneuve. Her mandate was to develop educational opportunities for aboriginal children and for the families of the French settlers in Ville-Marie.

Marguerite received the help of Jeanne Mance, founder of the Hôtel-Dieu Hospital. Other women joined her and the group formed an institute of uncloistered sisters, the Congregation of Notre-Dame. Marguerite and her companions took on many roles, including teaching, introducing vocational courses for youth and assisting couples preparing for marriage. She resisted Church pressure to change her community to a cloistered one and lived to see her order's rule confirmed in 1698. Marguerite died in 1700 at the age of 80 and was declared a saint on October 31, 1982. She is a patron saint of poor people.

Saint Joan of Arc

JOAN OF ARC (Jeanne d'Arc) was born in 1412 in Domrémy, France, during the Hundred Years' War. At an early age she received visions from St. Michael, St. Catherine and St. Margaret of Antioch, visions which would guide her throughout her short life. In 1429, following her "voices" to rid France of the English, Joan adopted male dress and led French forces in a successful assault against the English at Orléans, the most famous of her victories. Her success bred resentment among French Church authorities sympathetic to the English cause, leading in 1431 to her arrest for heresy, an ecclesiastical trial and subsequent burning at the stake.

Her conviction was annulled posthumously in 1456, and the Maid of Orléans soon became a French national symbol, culminating in her canonization in 1920. St. Joan's bravery, both in the face of battle and during her persecution by Church authorities, has made her a saint close to the hearts of women over the centuries.

When the pain is strong

When we must do something we dislike, let us say
to God, "My God I offer you this in honour
of the moment when you died for me."
—ST. JOHN MARY VIANNEY

Saint John Mary Vianney

THE NAME OF THIS FRENCH PRIEST may be unfamiliar to many, but his title is known around the world: the Curé of Ars. He was born in 1786 near Lyons, France. At age 20, he enrolled in school but found studying difficult. Having learned the rudiments of theology, John was ordained in 1815.

In 1818, John became the parish priest of the little village of Ars-en-Dombes, where most of the people were not interested in religion or God. He spent the rest of his life serving the parishioners of this village.

A renowned confessor, he was visited by hundreds of pilgrims every day, hearing confessions for 12 to 16 hours daily. When he walked from the confessional to the rectory, pilgrims would cut pieces from his clothing and his hair. For 30 years he served all who came to him: people were healed and converted, and many were given appropriate words of wisdom or advice even before they had explained their predicament. When he died in 1859 at the age of 73, John Vianney already had the reputation of being a saint. He was canonized in 1925 and is a patron of parish priests.

> *Consider everything before God; he will inspire you with the knowledge of what to do.*
>
> **–Bl. Élisabeth Turgeon**

Blessed Élisabeth Turgeon

Élisabeth Turgeon (1840-1881) founded the Sisters of Our Lady of the Holy Rosary (originally known as The Sisters of the Little Schools). She was born Beaumont, Quebec and studied in the Laval Normal School in Quebec City. She was a brilliant student and her diploma allowed her to teach in Lower Canada. Her career as a teacher was often interrupted by frail health, and poor health followed her on to Rimouski, where she arrived in 1875 at 35 years of age.

Élisabeth answered the repeated request of Bishop Jean Langevin, first Bishop of Rimouski, to join a group of women from the area who wanted to dedicate their lives to teaching in parochial schools. On September 12, 1879, the same day that they pronounced their vows, Élisabeth was named first superior of the Congregation of the Sisters of the Little Schools.

Sadly, her physical health was not up to the rigours of life as a teacher. Mother Élisabeth died August 17, 1881 in Rimouski at the age of 41. She was a woman of ardent faith, unrelenting courage, and tender and profound charity. Élisabeth Turgeon was declared Venerable in October 2013 and was beatified in Rimouski, Quebec, on April 26, 2015.

Without the burden of afflictions
it is impossible to reach the height of grace.
The gift of grace increases
as the struggle increases.
–St. Rose of Lima

Saint Rose of Lima

Saint Rose lived from 1586 to 1617. In 1671, she became the first canonized saint of the New World. Born in Lima, Peru, Rose embraced a life of prayer and penance while still a young girl, which she practised to the extreme, subjecting her body to austerities as well as deprivation of food and sleep. As a result, she endured interior periods of darkness and desolation as well as mystical experiences. She joined the Third Order of St. Dominic and lived in a little hut in her parents' garden, working to help support them by selling her needlework and flowers. St. Rosa is a patron of Peru and all of South America.

*We should abandon ourselves entirely
into the hands of God,
and believe that his providence disposes everything
that he wishes or permits to happen to us
for our greater good.*
—St. Vincent de Paul

Saint Vincent de Paul

SAINT VINCENT is the founder of the Congregation of the Missions (Vincentians) and co-founder of the Daughters of Charity. Born in France in 1580, the son of a peasant farmer, Vincent attended university and was ordained at 20. His first inclination was to earn a good income, but, appointed to the Queen's household, he came under the influence of Bérulle (later Cardinal), and became a changed man.

Vincent devoted the rest of his life to acts of charity. He organized groups to provide food and clothing for all who were poor: orphans, prostitutes, the sick, the disabled, the homeless. He established a congregation to preach and to train clergy. He collected large sums of money for his many projects and his influence spread from France across Europe. He died in 1660, was canonized in 1737 and is a patron saint of charitable societies.

> *Earth has no sorrow that heaven cannot heal.*
> —St. Thomas More

Saint Thomas More

THOMAS MORE was born in London in 1478. At 18, he was sent to study law and was called to the bar in 1501. Three years later he entered parliament. An enlightened man, he insisted that his three daughters receive the same education as his son.

Thomas' diverse achievements were recognized, and Cardinal Wolsey and the King wanted his services at court. In 1532, Wolsey was disgraced and Thomas replaced him as Lord Chancellor. He resigned three years later, openly opposing the king, as did John Fisher. With the passing of the Act of Succession in 1534, he was sought out and required to accept it. He refused twice and was imprisoned in the Tower of London. There he wrote the best of his spiritual works. Nine days after the death of John Fisher, Sir Thomas met the same death at the age of 57, claiming to be "the King's good servant, but God's first." St. Thomas is a patron of lawyers, statesmen and politicians.

> *You must believe in truth*
> *that whatever God gives or permits*
> *is for your salvation.*
> **—St. Catherine of Siena**

Saint Catherine of Siena

ONE OF FOUR WOMEN honoured with the title of Doctor of the Church, Catherine was born in Siena, Italy, in 1347, her parents' twenty-fifth and youngest child. At the age of seven, following a vision of Christ in glory, she is reported to have vowed her virginity to God. She joined the Dominican Third Order in 1365, spending years in seclusion from the world, fasting and praying. In 1368, after a vision where Christ accepted her as his "bride," she felt called to carry this love to others. She cared for the poor and tended the sick; she corresponded with people from all walks of life, even counselling princes and popes; she was renowned as a peacemaker. She is especially remembered for her spiritual reflections.

She died in Rome in 1380. This great Christian mystic was canonized in 1461, became a patron of Italy in 1939, and was declared a Doctor of the Church in 1970. She is co-patron of Europe with Sts. Benedict, Cyril and Methodius, Bridget of Sweden, and Teresa Benedicta of the Cross.

*If then you remain constant in your faith
in the face of trial,
the Lord will give you peace and rest
for a time in this world,
and forever in the next.*
—St. Jerome Emiliani

Saint Jerome Emiliani

JEROME WAS THE FOUNDER of the Somascan Fathers and Brothers, also known as the Company of the Servants of the Poor. Jerome was born in Venice in 1486. Initially, he pursued a career in the military and gave very little thought to God. After a conversion experience, however, he gave all his possessions to the poor, became a priest, and devoted himself to the instruction of orphans and troubled youth, and the care of the poor. He founded an order, the Somascan Fathers, to help with this work. One of his acquaintances was Pietro Carafa, who later became Pope Paul IV. Jerome died in 1537 of an illness contracted while tending the sick. He is a patron of orphans and abandoned children.

> *Nothing seems tiresome or painful*
> *when you are working for a Master who pays well;*
> *who rewards even a cup of cold water*
> *given for love of him.*
> **—St. Dominic Savio**

Saint Dominic Savio

BORN IN 1842 IN NORTHERN ITALY, Dominic Savio was a precocious boy. From an early age he showed great piety and devotion in practising his Catholic faith. For example, he received his First Communion at age seven when the accepted age was twelve – such was his deep understanding of his faith that an exception was made. When Dominic was twelve he was introduced to Fr. John Bosco who was impressed by Dominic's intelligence and piety and recommended he study in Turin at the Oratory of St. Francis de Sales under Fr. Bosco himself.

Although Dominic proved to be an exceptional student, his health was frail and he was sent home to recover. Sadly, his condition worsened and he died in 1857 at age fourteen. Fr. Bosco wrote a biography, "The Life of Dominic Savio," which brought the story of his brief life to a wide audience. Dominic Savio was canonized in 1854 and is a patron saint of choir boys.

*Fear is such a powerful emotion for humans
that when we allow it to take us over,
it drives compassion right out of our hearts.*
—St. Thomas Aquinas

Saint Thomas Aquinas

SAINT THOMAS AQUINAS was born near Aquino, Italy, about 1225. While his family was pious, they did not approve when 19-year-old Thomas joined the newly formed Dominicans, going so far as to imprison Thomas in the family castle. Once released, he studied in Italy and Germany, where, ironically, some of his classmates named this great thinker "the dumb ox," a name which prompted his teacher, Albert the Great, to proclaim: "We call him the dumb ox, but in his teaching he will one day produce such a bellowing that it will be heard throughout the world."

With Albert, he developed the theological Scholastic method, which dominated Catholic teaching for centuries. A prodigious writer, his most famous work is the *Summa theologica.* Many of his hymn texts, such as *Pange lingua, Tantum ergo* and *Adore te devote,* are still used today.

A man of towering intellect, Thomas was also a humble mystic. He died in 1274, was canonized in 1323, and declared a Doctor of the Church in 1567. In 1880, he was proclaimed a patron saint of universities and schools.

Searching for peace

> *Who except God can give you peace?*
> *Has the world ever been able*
> *to satisfy the heart?*
> —St. Gerard Majella

Saint Gerard Majella

GERARD MAJELLA was born in Muro, Italy in 1726. He grew up in poverty; when Gerard was twelve his father died and Gerard was sent away to apprentice as a tailor. Whatever he earned he shared with his mother and the poor, and devoted himself to prayer and fasting.

At the age of 23 Gerard entered the Redemptorists and three years later was professed as a lay brother. He worked tirelessly at manual labour, but was renown for his wise counsel and understanding, humility and generosity, with many people seeking him out for his sanctity and piety. He died in 1755 at the age of 29, having already been instrumental in miraculous cures in his lifetime. Gerard Majella was canonized in 1904 and is a patron of expectant mothers.

> *If we had no hope in the Lord,*
> *what would we do in this world?*
> **—St. Josephine Bakhita**

Saint Josephine Bakhita

JOSEPHINE WAS BORN IN 1869 in the Darfur region of western Sudan. She was sold as a slave several times until 1883, when she was sold to the Italian consul, who treated her with kindness and warmth. When he returned to Italy with his family, she accompanied them, and in 1888 she went to live at the Catechumenate of the Canossian Sisters in Venice. She was baptized in 1890, taking the name Josephine.

According to Italian law, since she had reached the age of majority, she was now free. She chose to join the Canossian Daughters of Charity and lived 50 years in religious life in Schio (Vicenza). She led a simple life as a cook, seamstress, and doorkeeper, and her gentleness and compassion for the poor and suffering endeared her to all.

Josephine died in 1947, after a long illness, and was canonized in 2000. The first saint from Sudan, St. Josephine Bakhita is the patron of that country.

> *God is love,*
> *and all his operations proceed from love.*
> —ST. LAWRENCE OF BRINDISI

Saint Lawrence of Brindisi

BORN IN 1559 IN THE KINGDOM OF NAPLES, Caesare de Rossi was educated first by the Conventual Friars and then in Venice at the College of Saint Mark. At the age of 16, he entered the Capuchin Franciscan Order in Verona and took the name Lawrence. Fluent in several languages, including Hebrew, and thoroughly versed in the Bible, Lawrence worked as a diplomat for the secular powers of Europe and as a missionary. In 1602, he became minister general of his order but refused re-election in 1605, preferring preaching to administration. He died in 1619.

Those who examined his writings in the process of his beatification became convinced that Lawrence deserved to be named a Doctor of the Church. He was canonized in 1881 and named Doctor of the Church in 1959.

> *God is not accustomed*
> *to refusing a good gift*
> *to those who ask for one.*
> **—St. Ambrose**

Saint Ambrose

AMBROSE WAS BORN INTO THE ARISTOCRACY in Trier, Germany, about 340, and served the powerful Roman Empire. As governor, he intervened in a dispute over the election of the bishop of Milan. Although he was only a catechumen, the laity elected him as bishop. He hesitated at first, but later was baptized and ordained. Ambrose became a remarkable preacher and teacher of the faith. His most famous student was Augustine of Hippo, whom he baptized. Ambrose died in 397. In 1298 he was declared one of the four great Doctors of the Latin Church (with Jerome, Augustine and Gregory I).

Those whose hearts are pure
are temples of the Holy Spirit.

−St. Lucy

Saint Lucy

LUCY WAS BORN IN SYRACUSE, Italy, and martyred about 304. Details of her life have been lost in the ensuing legends. During the Middle Ages, people suffering from eye trouble began invoking Lucy's aid because her name is derived from *lux* ('light'). St. Lucy is also associated with festivals of light, especially in Scandinavia.

Think well. Speak well. Do well.
These three things,
through the mercy of God,
will make a person go to heaven.
—St. Camillus de Lellis

Saint Camillus de Lellis

BORN IN ABRUZZI IN CENTRAL ITALY, Camillus (1550-1614) became a Venetian soldier like his father. When his father died, Camillus pursued his mania for gambling and lost everything; he ended up working at a Capuchin friary. Because of a diseased leg, he was unable to join that order, but found his vocation in caring for the sick. The conditions in hospitals in the 16th century were horrific and Camillus resolved to establish an order to care for the sick and dying.

Once ordained, he founded the nursing congregation of the Ministers of the Sick, the Camillians. Despite his own poor health, he served as general of his order, built hospitals and ministered to soldiers on the battlefield. Canonized in 1746, St. Camillus is a patron of nurses and of the sick.

We must often draw the comparison
between time and eternity.
This is the remedy of all our troubles.
How small will the present moment appear
when we enter that great ocean.
—St. Elizabeth Ann Seton

Saint Elizabeth Ann Seton

ELIZABETH ANN SETON is the first native-born American to be canonized. Born in 1774 in New York City into a wealthy family, at age 20 Elizabeth married William Seton and soon had a family of five young children. Sadly, she was widowed early in her marriage and found herself drawn to the Catholic faith as she sought to make sense of her crushing loss. After her conversion in 1805, Elizabeth was invited to set up Catholic girls schools, first in Baltimore and then in Emmetsburg, Maryland, considered to be the first Catholic parochial schools in the United States.

Elizabeth would go on to found the Sisters of Charity of St. Joseph, which grew to 20 communities by the time of her death in 1821. Mother Seton was canonized in 1975, and is a patron saint of widows and seafarers.

> *Peacefully do at each moment*
> *what at that moment ought to be done.*
> *We can trust God to take care of the master plan*
> *when we take care of the details.*
> —St. Katharine Drexel

Saint Katharine Drexel

KATHARINE DREXEL was born in 1858 into a wealthy family. The early death of her mother and the long illness and death of her stepmother were formative influences on Katharine. As well, a family trip into the western United States revealed to her the poor treatment and living conditions endured by indigenous peoples. Education and poverty would be issues close to her heart for the rest of her life.

After her father's death in 1885, she started to use her large inheritance to improve the lot of African Americans in the South and indigenous Americans in the West. In 1889, she joined the Sisters of Mercy and subsequently founded the Sisters of the Blessed Sacrament in order to devote her life and wealth to serving Americans on the margins. By the time of her death in 1955, there were 500 Sisters in 51 convents, and dozens of schools had been set up all across the United States.

Katharine Drexel was canonized in 1975, the second American-born saint (after St. Elizabeth Ann Seton). She is a patron of racial justice and philanthropists.

The world cannot give up its dream of universal peace.
It is precisely because peace is always coming to be,
always incomplete, always fragile, always under
attack, always difficult, that we proclaim it.
We proclaim it as a duty, an inescapable duty.
—St. Paul VI

Saint Paul VI

Giovanni Battista Montini was born in 1897 in Italy. Ordained in 1920, he was appointed Archbishop of Milan in 1953 and became known as the "archbishop of the workers." Pope John XXIII named Montini a cardinal in 1958 and soon after announced the Second Vatican Council. During the Council, however, Pope John XXIII died, and the well-respected Montini was elected on June 21, 1963, to succeed him, taking the name Paul VI. He continued the Council, implementing reforms in liturgy, Church governance, and the attitudes of Catholics toward other religions. Though controversies surrounding ideas and encyclicals, especially 1968's *Humanae vitae,* can be seen as overshadowing his pontificate, the reality is that Paul VI's papacy brought a message of human rights, human dignity and human development to the world.

Paul VI died on August 6, 1978. He was beatified on October 19, 2014, and canonized on October 14, 2018. *(sources: slmedia.org; vatican.va)*

God's mercy lifts me up

Let not the things,
which have been made new,
return to their ancient instability.
—ST. LEO THE GREAT

Saint Leo the Great

LEO WAS BORN TO TUSCAN PARENTS. His religious beliefs guided his entire life. As a deacon he worked to bring peace to warring Roman factions who were leaving Gaul vulnerable to barbarian invasion. Leo is well known for his peacekeeping efforts, and especially for his encounter with Attila the Hun, persuading Attila not to plunder Rome. During another attack three years later, Leo was not so successful, though he did manage to save the city from being burnt. Leo worked alongside the people to rebuild the city and its churches.

Pope from 440 until his death in 461, Leo is best known for his sermons on faith and charity. Always a strong opponent of heresies, his teaching has had a lasting influence on the life of the Roman Church.

St. Leo the Great is the first pope whose sermons and letters have been preserved in extensive collections. He was made Doctor of the Church in 1754.

To be taken with love for a soul,
God does not look on its greatness,
but the greatness of its humility.

—St. John of the Cross

Saint John of the Cross

JOHN WAS BORN IN 1542 at Fontiveros, Spain. He entered the Carmelite community and was ordained in 1567. With the great Carmelite mystic, Teresa of Avila, he worked for the reformation of his order, and helped found the reformed ('Discalced') Carmelites.

During his life, John suffered much, enduring imprisonment, humiliation and ill-treatment. His writings are both classics of spirituality and of Spanish literature. His best-known works are *The Ascent of Mount Carmel, The Dark Night of the Soul,* and *The Living Flame of Love.* He died in 1591, was canonized in 1726 and proclaimed Doctor of the Church in 1926. St. John of the Cross is a patron of contemplatives.

Live on the divine Eucharist,
like the Hebrews did on the Manna.
Your soul can be entirely dedicated to the divine
Eucharist and very holy in the midst of your work
and contacts with the world.

—St. Peter Julian Eymard

Saint Peter Julian Eymard

SAINT PETER JULIAN EYMARD was born in 1811 near Grenoble, France. Ordained as a diocesan priest in 1834, he later transferred to the Marists and in 1851 confided to his superior a call he felt to establish a group of men dedicated to adoration of the Blessed Sacrament. By 1863 Rome had approved the Congregation of the Blessed Sacrament, whose charism is to promote the significance of the Eucharist for Christian living. Eymard also founded a community for religious women.

Eymard believed that both prayer and works of charity are essential to the priestly life. Accordingly, the congregation worked with the very poor, preparing them to receive communion, but also caring for their material needs.

Eymard is considered a pioneer in the rediscovery of the importance of the "bread of life" and in his call to involve laypersons more actively in the life of the Church. He died in 1868 and was canonized in 1962 by Pope John XXIII.

> *The rivers of grace cannot flow uphill,*
> *up the steep cliff of the proud person's heart.*
> —St. Bernard of Clairvaux

Saint Bernard of Clairvaux

SAINT BERNARD was born near Dijon, France in 1090. In his *Apologia,* he wrote that it was because of his unruly nature that he chose the newly founded Cistercians, thinking their austerity could tame him.

At 22, Bernard went to Cîteaux, an abbey known for its strict observance of St. Benedict's Rule. His remarkable enthusiasm helped persuade his uncle, his brothers and many friends to join him. A group of about 30 men left for the abbey. Within three years, Bernard was sent with 12 monks to a diocese in Champagne where, in a valley that came to be known as the Valley of Light ("Clairvaux"), Bernard founded the monastery where he ruled as abbot for the rest of his life.

From the time he became abbot until his death in 1153, Bernard dominated the religious and political life of Western Europe. His writings have had a lasting influence on Catholic spirituality and his abbey became the motherhouse for dozens of Cistercian monasteries around the world.

When Bernard died, Europe mourned. He was canonized in 1174 and declared a Doctor of the Church in 1830.

We are not the sum of our weaknesses and failures;
we are the sum of the Father's love for us and our real
capacity to become the image of his Son Jesus.
—St. John Paul II

Saint John Paul II

Karol Józef Wojtyła, known as John Paul II since his October 1978 election to the papacy, was born in Poland in 1920. He was ordained to the priesthood in 1946, made bishop in 1958, archbishop in 1964 and cardinal in 1967.

After the death of Pope John Paul I in 1978, the cardinals elected him Pope and he took the name of John Paul II.

In 1984, John Paul II became the first Pope to step foot on Canadian soil when he launched a 12-day pastoral visit. In June 1987, John Paul II returned to Canada to meet with the people of Fort Simpson, Northwest Territories. During his first visit in 1984, severe weather conditions had prevented him from meeting with Aboriginal Peoples from the North. However, he had promised to return, which he did in 1987.

John Paul II's pontificate, one of the longest in the history of the Church, lasted nearly 27 years. He died on April 2, 2005, the vigil of Divine Mercy Sunday. John Paul II was canonized on April 27, 2014. Saint John Paul II is the patron saint of World Youth Day. *(sources: slmedia.org; vatican.va)*

Saint Francis Xavier

FRANCIS WAS BORN IN 1506 in Navarre, Spain. He met St. Ignatius of Loyola at the University of Paris, and was one of the first members of the Society of Jesus (Jesuits). Francis spent many years working as a missionary with the peoples of Goa, Southeast Asia and Japan. He had excellent organizational skills: the communities he established continued to flourish long after his departure. Francis died while on his way from Goa to China, in 1552. He was canonized in 1602 and is a patron of all foreign missions.

> *The devil may try to use the hurts of life to make you feel it is impossible that Jesus really loves you. This is completely the opposite of what Jesus is really wanting, waiting to tell you... he loves you always, even when you don't feel worthy.*
>
> —St. Teresa of Calcutta

Saint Teresa of Calcutta

AGNES GONXHA BOJAXHIU was born in Skopje (in what is now Northern Macedonia) in 1910. She joined the Institute of the Blessed Virgin Mary (Loretto sisters) in Ireland in 1928 and took the name Sister Mary Teresa. The next year she was assigned to Calcutta, and from the time of her final profession in 1937 was known as Mother Teresa.

It was during a train ride in 1946 that Mother Teresa received a vision and an invitation to serve the poorest of the poor – what she described as her "call within a call." She moved to the slums and began serving people on the margins of Indian society. Soon, others were drawn to join her, and she founded the Missionaries of Charity in 1948.

During her long life, Mother Teresa became known to people all over the world, with her community established in more than 90 countries. Mother Teresa died in Calcutta in 1997 and was canonized in 2016. St. Teresa of Calcutta is the patron saint of World Youth Day.

It is not those who commit the least faults who are most holy, but those who have the greatest courage, the greatest generosity, the greatest love, who make the boldest efforts to overcome themselves, and are not immoderately apprehensive of tripping.

—ST. FRANCIS DE SALES

Saint Francis de Sales

A LEADER OF THE CATHOLIC REFORMATION, Francis was born in France in 1567. His family insisted he study law rather than enter the seminary. After obtaining doctorates in both canon and civil law by the age of 24, Francis chose religious life instead. His family eventually became reconciled to his choice and he was ordained in 1593.

Appointed bishop of Geneva in 1602, Francis reorganized the diocese, reformed religious education, established a seminary and founded schools. He lived a life of austerity and simplicity, sharing with the poor. Wise and intelligent, he emphasized both the loving kindness of God and the human capacity for love.

Francis was beatified the year he died, 1622 – the first formal beatification to take place in St. Peter's – and canonized in 1665. St. Francis de Sales is the patron saint of writers and journalists, and of the deaf.

Mary, Mother of God

*If you put all the love of all the mothers
into one heart
it still would not equal
the love of the heart of Mary
for her children.*

—St. Louis Grignion de Montfort

Saint Louis Grignion de Montfort

BORN IN SAINT-MALO, France, Louis Grignion (1673-1716) was the founder of the Company of Mary, the Daughters of Wisdom and the Brothers of Saint Gabriel. Ordained in 1700, he was first appointed chaplain to a hospital in Poitiers. While his introduction of much-needed reforms led to the beginning of a congregation for women staff members, it also stirred up resentment, and he was forced to leave. He began instead to preach missions for the poor. Again, his success caused resentment and he was forced to stop.

He left on foot for Rome and received from the Pope the title of "missionary apostolic." For the rest of his life he preached and gave missions. He died at the age of 43, having just begun to form his association of ordained men, the Missionaries of the Company of Mary. He was canonized in 1947.

My confidence in our good Mother is unlimited.
She knows our needs
and has such great power
over the heart of her divine Son.
—BL. MARIE-LÉONIE PARADIS

Blessed Marie-Léonie Paradis

ÉLODIE PARADIS was born in 1840 in L'Acadie, Quebec. At age 17 she took vows with the Marianite Sisters, a branch of the Congregation of Holy Cross. She taught in Montreal, New York and Indiana before finding the opportunity to fulfill her calling of dedication to the care of priests and seminarians. In 1877, Mother Marie-Léonie (Élodie's religious name), with 14 young Acadian women, founded the Little Sisters of the Holy Family, in Memramcook, New Brunswick.

Mother Marie-Léonie worked tirelessly for others and was known for her generosity and humility. She died in 1912 and was beatified by Pope John Paul II in 1984.

> *When you see the storm coming,*
> *if you seek safety in that firm refuge*
> *which is Mary,*
> *there will be no danger*
> *of your wavering*
> *or going down.*
> —St. Josemaría Escrivá

Saint Josemaría Escrivá

Josemaría Escrivá de Balaguer (1902-1975) was born in Barbastro, Spain and ordained in 1925. He worked as a pastor in Madrid until moving to Rome in 1946. During this period in Spain, which was interrupted by a period in hiding during the Spanish Civil War, Josemaría received a vision leading him to found Opus Dei, a society dedicated to the sanctification of everyday life. It received papal approval as a secular institute in 1950, and today can be found in more than 60 countries. Josemaría was canonized in 2002.

In trial or difficulty I have recourse to Mother Mary,
whose glance alone is enough to dissipate every fear.
—St. Thérèse of Lisieux

Saint Thérèse of Lisieux

Marie-Françoise Thérèse Martin was born in Normandy, France, in 1873, the youngest of nine. Her mother died when Thérèse was only five years old and the family moved to Lisieux, where she was raised by her father, her sisters and an aunt. Three of her sisters became Carmelite nuns and the fourth joined the Visitandines.

Thérèse entered the Carmel of Lisieux when she was 15. Her motto was a phrase from the great Carmelite mystic, John of the Cross: "Love is repaid by love alone." Thérèse held special devotions to the heart of Jesus and to the spiritual Motherhood of Mary. She pioneered the ideal of the "little way": fidelity in the small things, trust and complete self-surrender to God.

Thérèse had a gift for writing, and the prioress, her sister Pauline, directed her to write first about her childhood, then about her life in the convent. These were combined into *The Story of a Soul,* a modern spiritual autobiography.

Known popularly as The Little Flower, Thérèse died in 1897. Though Thérèse's life spanned only 24 years, her faith and simplicity were remarkable. She was canonized in 1925 and made Doctor of the Church in 1997. St. Thérèse of Lisieux is a patron of missions.

The Rosary is the most beautiful
and the most rich in graces of all prayers;
it is the prayer that touches most
the heart of the Mother of God.

−St. Pius X

Saint Pius X

GIUSEPPE SARTO was born in Riese, Italy, in 1835. His mother was a seamstress and his father a parish clerk who died when Giuseppe was 16, leaving the family in financial straits. His mother insisted that the boy continue his education and fulfill his desire to become a priest. Ordained at 23, he was involved in pastoral ministry for 17 years. He became a bishop in 1884, a cardinal in 1892 and was elected pope in 1903. He died in 1914, soon after the outbreak of World War I.

His recommendations and encyclicals reflect his pastoral background: he advocated frequent communion for adults, sacramental preparation for children and instruction in catechism for everyone. In his concern for the Church in a rapidly changing world, he issued a decree against writers holding modernist ideas in philosophy and theology and wrote an encyclical condemning modernism in all its manifestations. St. Pius X was canonized in 1954.

> *Seek refuge in Mary*
> *because she is the city of refuge.*
> **—ST. ANTHONY OF PADUA**

Saint Anthony of Padua

ANTHONY was born in 1195 in Lisbon, Portugal, although the Italian city of Padua claims him as its own. At 15, he joined the Canons Regular of Saint Augustine. For eight years he studied intensely, becoming an accomplished biblical scholar. His contact with some Franciscans inspired him to join their community. He was sent by Francis to preach and to teach his fellow friars throughout northern Italy, first in Bologna and then in Padua. His reputation drew enormous crowds, and the power of his words converted them. Ill and exhausted, he died at the age of 36; so beloved and revered, he was canonized within the year. St. Anthony of Padua's aid is invoked to help find lost objects.

> *People do not fear a powerful hostile army*
> *as the powers of hell*
> *fear the name and protection of Mary.*
>
> —ST. BONAVENTURE

Saint Bonaventure

BORN IN 1221 IN TUSCANY and baptized as Giovanni, legend has it that, while a child, he was given the name Bonaventure ("Good Fortune") by Saint Francis of Assisi, who cured him miraculously of a dangerous illness. Bonaventure joined the Friars Minor at age 20 and was sent to the University of Paris. Thomas Aquinas was his friend and colleague; the two received their doctorates of theology at the same time.

Pope Gregory X, preparing an ecumenical council at Lyons designed to reunite the Greek and Latin rites, called on Thomas and Bonaventure to assist him. Thomas Aquinas died on the way to the Council and at the end of it, Bonaventure, who had been the predominant figure at the assembly, also died. Despite his reputation for holiness, humility and virtue, his canonization was delayed until 1482 because of dissension within the Franciscan Order. In 1588, he was declared a Doctor of the Church. Bonaventure's writings such as his *Life of Saint Francis* as well as on history, spirituality and medieval mystical doctrine, still inspire readers.

> *There is no problem, I tell you,*
> *no matter how difficult it is,*
> *that we cannot resolve*
> *by the prayer of the Holy Rosary.*
> —SERVANT OF GOD LÚCIA DOS SANTOS OF FATIMA

Servant of God Lúcia dos Santos of Fatima

LÚCIA DOS SANTOS OF FATIMA (1907-2005) was born near Fatima, Portugal into a family of seven children. In 1917, she and two of her cousins, Francisco and Jacinto, received apparitions of the Blessed Virgin Mary over a six-month period. The messages they received from Our Lady were quickly publicized, resulting in an official investigation into the apparitions in 1922. By 1930 the local bishop had authorized the veneration of Our Lady of Fatima, which has led to Fatima being one of the Catholic Church's great pilgrimage sights. Lúcia's cousins died soon after the apparitions, and Lúcia became a Carmelite nun in 1949, taking the name Sister Maria Lúcia of Jesus of the Immaculate Heart. She died in 2005 and was declared Servant of God in 2017, the first step on the path to sainthood.

*Trust all things to Jesus in the Blessed Sacrament
and to Mary, help of Christians,
and you will see what miracles are.*
—St. John Bosco

Saint John Bosco

Known to many as Don Bosco, this patron saint of youth was born in Piedmont, Italy in 1815. Raised in poverty, John was ordained in Turin in 1841. After witnessing the circumstances of boys living in a local prison, he resolved to devote himself to working among disadvantaged boys – children living on the street, juvenile delinquents and any child who was suffering because of disadvantage.

He formed the Salesian Society, named after Francis de Sales, and began holding evening classes in factories, in fields or wherever there was a need. A progressive thinker, he abhorred all punishment, believing that by removing youth from temptation, treating them with dignity and kindness, and enriching them with skills, they could be led to more productive lives. His rule was, "Not with blows, but with charity and gentleness must you draw these friends to the path of virtue." With the help of Saint Mary Mazzarello, he also established the Salesian Sisters to do similar work among girls. John Bosco died in 1888 and was canonized in 1934.

*Loving God
and neighbour*

*It is not hard to obey
when we love the one whom we obey.*

—St. Ignatius of Loyola

Saint Ignatius of Loyola

IGNATIUS OF LOYOLA (1491-1556) was born in northern Spain and raised as a gentleman destined for military service. In 1521, during the defence of Pamplona, he was struck by a cannonball. As he convalesced, he read a life of Christ and lives of the saints and found himself inflamed with the desire to serve Jesus.

Leaving home, Ignatius spent a vigil at Mary's altar in the Benedictine monastery of Montserrat and then lived in the nearby town of Manresa, praying and serving the poor. During this time, he had mystical experiences and illuminations, which later formed the basis of his Spiritual Exercises. After a brief stay in the Holy Land, Ignatius returned to Europe and gathered together a group of students, including Francis Xavier, with whom he shared his eagerness for whole-hearted service of Jesus. He brought the group to Rome, where they offered themselves in service to the pope and formed the Society of Jesus (Jesuits).

Ignatius spent the rest of his life directing the rapidly growing order, writing its constitutions and refining the Spiritual Exercises. He was canonized in 1622 and is a universal patron of retreats and soldiers.

They who sow courtesy
reap friendship,
and they who plant kindness
gather love.

—St. Basil the Great

Saint Basil the Great

Born in the province of Cappadocia in Asia Minor about 330, Basil came from a deeply Christian family. Baptized in his late twenties, he decided in 358 to live as a hermit. So many joined him that he established a form of ascetic life lived in common. His writings gave rise to the tradition of Byzantine monasticism which later influenced Saint Benedict.

In 370, Basil was appointed archbishop of Caesarea and led the battle in the East against the Arian heresy. Considered one of the great orators of Christian history, he is also one of the four great Doctors of the Eastern Church (with Gregory Nazianzen, Athanasius and John Chrysostom), and is the patron saint of hospital administrators.

> *May Jesus Christ Our Lord be forever*
> *the sole possessor of our hearts,*
> *as he will be,*
> *if we love and seek only him in all things.*
> —St. Marie of the Incarnation

Saint Marie of the Incarnation

The first missionary woman to the New World, Marie was born in Tours, France, in 1599. Denying her own attraction to religious life, Marie honoured her father's wishes and married Claude Martin in 1617. Claude died only three years later. Soon after, Marie began receiving revelations concerning the Incarnation, the Sacred Heart and the Blessed Trinity. After seeking spiritual direction, she entered the Ursuline monastery in Tours.

Encouraged by a dream, she set sail with two other Ursulines, arriving in Quebec City in 1639. There, they opened their first school in Lowertown. The school grew despite sickness, poverty and strained relations with the Native peoples. When the Québecois were threatened by tensions with the Iroquois nation, Marie was recalled to France but she chose to remain in New France. She composed catechisms in Huron and Algonquin, and a dictionary of French and Algonquin. Marie died in Quebec in 1672. She was beatified in 1980 and canonized in 2014.

If you truly want to help the soul of your neighbour,
you should approach God first with all your heart.
Ask him simply to fill you with charity,
the greatest of all virtues;
with it you can accomplish what you desire.
—St. Vincent Ferrer

Saint Vincent Ferrer

A PATRON OF BUILDERS, ROOFERS AND PLUMBERS, Vincent was born in Spain in 1350. He joined the Dominicans in 1367, who sent him to study and teach philosophy throughout Europe. Despite his stern interpretation of the Christian message, Vincent became an amazingly successful preacher, converting thousands. He was also a key figure in ending the Western Schism, a divide in the Church over pretenders to the papacy. He died in 1419 and was canonized in 1455.

> *Peace and union are the most necessary of all things*
> *for people who live in common,*
> *and nothing serves so well*
> *to establish and maintain these*
> *as the forbearing charity*
> *whereby we put up with one another's defects.*
> —ST. ROBERT BELLARMINE

Saint Robert Bellarmine

SAINT ROBERT BELLARMINE is one of the Church's great apologists. Born in Tuscany, Italy, in 1542, he entered the Jesuits in 1560 and was renowned for his preaching even before his ordination in 1570. After years of study and teaching, he was made Professor of Controversial Theology at the Roman College.

Robert's many roles included reviser of the Latin Vulgate Bible, advisor to Galileo, author of two catechisms, leader in the Catholic Reformation, head of the Vatican library, and theological consultant to the Holy See.

Appointed cardinal in 1599 and archbishop of Capua in 1602, he was greatly loved as a pastor. He died in 1621, was canonized in 1930 and declared a Doctor of the Church in 1931. St. Robert Bellarmine is a patron of catechists and catechumens.

If the poison of pride is swelling up in you,
turn to the Eucharist;
and that Bread,
which is your God
humbling and disguising himself,
will teach you humility.
—St. Cyril of Alexandria

Saint Cyril of Alexandria

CYRIL WAS A PATRIARCH OF THE EASTERN CHURCH and a Greek theologian. In 412, he succeeded his uncle as archbishop of Alexandria and used his power and wealth to champion his cause – the defence of the doctrines of the Church. At the Council of Ephesus in 431 in the great christological controversy against Nestorius, Cyril held that the relationship between the divine and human in Christ was so closely united that the Virgin was actually *Theotokos* (Mother of God). This controversy engaged Cyril until his death in 444. In 1882, St. Cyril of Alexandria was declared a Doctor of the Church.

Imitation is not a literal mimicking of Christ;
rather, it means becoming the image of the beloved,
an image disclosed through transformation.
This means we are to become vessels
of God's compassionate love for others.

−St. Clare

Saint Clare

SAINT CLARE WAS BORN IN ASSISI about the year 1193. At the age of 18 she heard a sermon by Francis of Assisi and committed herself to a life of poverty. On Passion Sunday 1212, she secretly left home and went to the place where Francis lived with his community. She received the habit from him and went to live in a nearby Benedictine convent.

Clare was joined by others, and the small community moved to San Damiano, near Assisi. In 1215, Clare was made abbess of the Poor Clares. The women modelled their life on the ideals of St. Francis. They did without shoes, slept on the ground and never ate meat. Before long, other houses were founded in several countries.

Clare received papal approval for her own Rule the day before she died − the first rule for religious life written by a woman for women. She was credited with many miracles and canonized just two years after her death. St. Clare of Assisi is a patron saint of eye diseases and television.

Be honourable
so that you may never
voluntarily bring disgrace
upon anyone.
–St. Stephen of Hungary

Saint Stephen of Hungary

SAINT STEPHEN and his father, the third duke to govern the Magyars, were baptized when Stephen was ten. In 997, when he was 22, Stephen succeeded his father and was soon at war in his attempt to unite the Magyars. Having consolidated his position, Stephen obtained Pope Sylvester II's approval for the proper establishment of the Church in Hungary. Stephen was crowned first King of Hungary in 1001.

Stephen ensured that Magyars were trained as priests, churches were built, and the great monastery of St. Martin, begun by his father, was finished. He instituted reforms in religion, civil law and government.

A deeply committed Christian, Stephen was very generous, often distributing alms. When his only son died in a hunting accident, Stephen's life was made miserable by fights over the succession. He died in 1038, having united Hungary in politics and in religion, and was canonized in 1083.

> *Loving Heart of our Lord Jesus Christ,*
> *you move hearts that are harder than rock,*
> *you melt spirits that are colder than ice,*
> *and you reach souls*
> *that are more impenetrable*
> *than diamonds.*
>
> —ST. MARGARET MARY ALACOQUE

Saint Margaret Mary Alacoque

MARGARET WAS BORN IN 1647 in Burgundy, France. At 14, having been cured of a lengthy illness, she decided to become a nun. It was not until 1671, however, that she was able to enter the Visitation convent at Paray-le-Monial. Between 1673 and 1676 she experienced four visions concerning the Sacred Heart, and was told to record them by her confessor, the brilliant Jesuit Claude la Colombière.

By 1686 the community too was honouring the heart of Jesus, and in 1688 a chapel in the garden was consecrated to the Sacred Heart. Two years later Margaret died, but the devotion she had begun at Paray was now firmly established. She was canonized in 1920 and is the patron of devotees to the Sacred Heart.

Building a just world

> *Do something, get moving,*
> *risk new things, stick with it,*
> *get on your knees,*
> *then be ready for big surprises.*
> —St. Angela Merici

Saint Angela Merici

Born in 1474 in Desenzano, Italy, into a happy rural home, Angela was orphaned in her teens. As she matured, pilgrim journeys and life-giving relationships with many people helped her to discover her vocation. On November 25, 1535, 28 women promised their lives to God as members of the Company of St. Ursula (an early Christian leader of women). Angela had developed a way of life or a Rule based on her experience as a single lay woman, allowing each member to respond to societal needs according to her gifts, thus creating a freer, more independent and yet committed life for women.

Angela Merici died in 1540. The 1600s saw the development of the Ursuline Order, focusing on the education of young women. Both the Company of St. Ursula and the Ursuline Order subsequently spread throughout Italy, the rest of Europe and the world. Angela Merici was canonized in 1807 and is a patron of the sick and orphans.

> *Consult not your fears*
> *but your hopes and your dreams.*
> *Concern yourself not with what you tried and failed in,*
> *but with what is still possible for you to do.*
> **–St. John XXIII**

Saint John XXIII

POPE JOHN XXIII was born Angelo Giuseppe Roncalli in 1881. In 1904 he was ordained a priest and served as seminary teacher, sergeant in the medical corps, military chaplain, spiritual director, and Apostolic Visitor before being appointed bishop in 1925. In 1953 he was created a cardinal and sent to Venice as patriarch.

At the death of Pius XII he was elected pope on October 28, 1958, taking the name John XXIII. His pontificate, which lasted less than five years, presented him to the entire world as an authentic image of the Good Shepherd.

He convoked the Roman Synod, established the Commission for the Revision of the Code of Canon Law and summoned the Second Vatican Council. His social magisterium in the encyclicals *Pacem in terris* and *Mater et magistra* was deeply appreciated.

Pope John XXIII died in 1963. He was canonized in 2014, along with Saint John Paul II. *(source: slmedia.org)*

And let them first pray together,
that so they may associate in peace.
—St. Benedict

Saint Benedict

Benedict, Father of Western monasticism, lived circa 480 to 547. He was born in Nursia in central Italy. The little we know of his personal life comes from the second *Dialogue* of Gregory the Great, and the Rule written by Benedict himself.

Benedict was educated in Rome. After a few years, convinced that God was calling him to be a monk or hermit, Benedict fled to a local village. After a brief stay with some holy men, he decided on a life of solitude, retiring to a cave where he lived alone in the tradition of the Desert Fathers. Soon, he began to attract followers.

Between 520 and 530, he and a few companions founded the great monastery of Monte Cassino, where Benedict spent the rest of his life and wrote his Rule. This work became the primary influence on Western religious life for the next 600 years. This remarkable guide reflects the fatherly concern and charity of Benedict as he adapted the austere rule of the Desert Fathers to community life. He emphasized moderation, humility, obedience, prayer and manual labour as the way to holiness. Saint Benedict was canonized in 1220, is considered the Patriarch of Western Monasticism, and was proclaimed a patron of Europe in 1964 by Pope Paul VI.

If you have those who will exclude any of God's creatures from the shelter of compassion and pity, you will have those who will deal likewise with their brothers and sisters.

—St. Francis of Assisi

Saint Francis of Assisi

FRANCESCO BERNARDONE was born in Assisi, Italy circa 1181. The son of a wealthy silk merchant, Francis lived a life of comfort and pleasure. Believing his call was to serve God and the poor, he chose the way of poverty and self-denial. In 1209 he understood that his work was to build up the Church by preaching repentance. His zeal won disciples, and in 1210 a Rule was approved, with the Pope giving Francis and his companions a commission to preach. By 1219, they numbered 5,000.

Francis is credited with creating the first crèche, in 1223, to mark Christmas. Francis is also recognized as being the first to teach that the earth itself is holy.

A deacon all his life, Francis' visionary leadership inspired thousands to lead lives of poverty, simplicity and humble service, delighting in creation and consumed with love for Christ. Francis died at Assisi on October 3, 1226 and was canonized two years later. St. Francis of Assisi is a patron of Italy and of ecologists.

No act is charitable if it is not just.

−St. Bruno

Saint Bruno

Bruno, founder of the Carthusian Order, was born in Cologne, Germany, about 1030. He studied at Rheims and was invited back to teach theology and grammar. During his 18 years at Rheims he taught many eminent scholars and was chancellor of the diocese. When the Archbishop died in 1068, his replacement was highly unsuitable and the objections of Bruno and other canons were met with persecution, which forced them to flee the city. Eventually that Archbishop was deposed.

Clerical corruption left Bruno wanting to live a contemplative life. In 1080 he gave up his riches and, with six companions, began to live as a hermit. In 1084, the group was granted land in the Chartreuse Mountains. This was the beginning of the Carthusian Order and of the great abbey that is its motherhouse.

In recognition of his great learning, Bruno was called to Rome in 1090 to assist the Pope, a former pupil. It was soon obvious that Bruno was not suited to court life and he was permitted to found a second monastery in Calabria, close enough to be available to the Holy See. He died there in 1101, leaving no rule, but a spirit of prayerful simplicity, which lives on. While never officially canonized, his feast was added to the Roman Calendar in 1623. St. Bruno is patron of Calabria.

May Christ be heard in our language,
may Christ be seen in our life,
may he be perceived in our hearts.
—St. Peter Damian

Saint Peter Damian

SAINT PETER DAMIAN is a Doctor of the Church, so honoured for his writings, as well as his work for reform and renewal of the Church.

Peter was born in 1007 into a large family in Ravenna, Italy. He was orphaned at a very young age, and the first brother to care for him treated him very badly. Another brother, however, a priest in Ravenna, recognized Peter's brilliance and arranged for schooling. Peter appreciated this so much that he took on his brother's name and called himself Peter Damian. He became a hermit monk and was eventually chosen as the superior of his community. In 1057 he was appointed the bishop of Ostia.

Throughout his life he fought for clerical reform and against the laxness and immorality of the clergy of his day. Eventually, he received permission from Pope Alexander to return to the simple life of a monk. He died in 1072 and, while never formally canonized, St. Peter Damian was declared Doctor of the Church in 1828.

*Arise, soldiers of Christ, throw away the works
of darkness and put on the armour of light.*
−St. Cecilia

Saint Cecilia

Legend claims that a Roman woman named Cecilia was martyred for the faith sometime in the second or third century, a few days after her husband Valerian and his brother Tiburtius were beheaded for refusing to sacrifice to the gods. Her association with music – she is a patron saint of musicians – stems from the story that at her wedding feast she sang to God in her heart.

Honoured since the early years of the Church, St. Cecilia is mentioned in the list of saints in the first Eucharistic Prayer.

We who have a voice must speak for the voiceless.
—St. Óscar Romero

Saint Óscar Romero

Óscar Romero (1917-1980) was Archbishop of San Salvador. He was assassinated on March 24, 1980 as he was celebrating Mass in the chapel of the hospital where he lived. In 2015 he was beatified and declared a martyr of the Church. On October 14, 2018 he was canonized by Pope Francis.

In 2015 Pope Francis wrote to the Archbishop of San Salvador on the occasion of Romero's beatification: "In the beautiful land of Central America [...] the Lord granted his Church a zealous bishop who, loving God and serving brothers and sisters, became the image of Christ the Good Shepherd. In times of difficult coexistence, Archbishop Romero knew how to lead, defend and protect his flock, remaining faithful to the Gospel and in communion with the whole Church. His ministry was distinguished by particular attention to the most poor and marginalized. And at the moment of his death, while he celebrated the Holy Sacrifice of love and reconciliation, he received the grace to identify himself fully with the One who gave his life for his sheep." St. Óscar has been described as "a martyr of the Church of the Second Vatican Council" because he chose "to live with the poor to defend them from oppression." (Archbishop Vincenzo Paglia)

♈Livingwith**Christ**

Published in Canada
   by Novalis

Publisher:
Jonathan Guilbault

Editor:
Natalia Kononenko
natalia.kononenko@novalis.ca

Associate Editor:
Nancy Keyes

Layout and Design:
Jessica Llewellyn

Business Office:
Novalis, Periodicals Dept.
1 Eglinton Avenue East, Suite 800
Toronto, ON M4P 3A1
tel: (416) 363-3303
fax: (416) 363-9409
email: living@novalis.ca
www.livingwithchrist.ca

ISBN: 978-2-89830-017-2

Printed in Canada

Published in the United States
   by Bayard, Inc.

Publisher:
Joseph Sinasac

Associate Publisher:
Richard Lamoureux, AA

Editor:
Terence Hegarty
terence.hegarty@bayard-inc.com

Business Office:
Bayard, Inc.
One Montauk Ave, Suite 200
New London, CT 06320
tel: 1-800-321-0411
www.livingwithchrist.us

ISBN: 978-1-62785-728-4

Cover photos: iStock, Dreamstime, Shutterstock
Interior photos: iStock: p. 2, 12, 22, 32, 51, 61, 71, Dreamstime: p. 42